Gratitude is the healthiest
of all human emotions.
The more you express gratitude
for what you have,
the more likely you will
have even more to express
gratitude for.

Zig Ziglar

Gratitude is one of many positive emotions. It's about focusing on what's good in our lives and being thankful for the things we have. Gratitude is pausing to notice and appreciate the things that we often take for granted, like the people around us, having a place to live, food, clean water, friends, family, and a purpose to live by.

By recording those moments when we particularly appreciate the action or words of others, or when the universe responds to our needs in a particularly special way, we can draw strength from them in moments when we need to be reminded of what a wonderful world we live in. Use this book to capture all of life's special moments and gifts. In the future, when you may be feeling less strong and in need of inspiration, you can refer back to it and regain your strength.

About Moses

Moses opened his first business when he was only 23 years old. Since then, he has mastered the skill of High-Performance Coaching and has been helping his clients to level up in life and businesses by removing self-sabotaging beliefs and helping them solve burning problems.

In 2019 he went to Bulgaria to represent and develop the market for Tony Robbins and Success Resources. Back in the day, Moses broke all sales records for Success Resources as a Business Mastery leading consultant using High-Performance Coaching Skills. Now, Moses is on a mission to train 1000 new coaches and trainers by 2025 through his Upper Echelon Coaching Academy.

He has worked closely with some of the most admired people in business and self-actualization, such as Robert Kiyosaki, Gary Vaynerchuk, and Tony Robbins, to name a few.

He has trained the leaders of Philip Morris International, TechoArena, Transpress, iBrokers, FitLine, Oriflame, Entegra, BulMed Consulting, Happy Bar and Grill, and UXP, as well as coaching the Bulgarian Olympic Gold Medalist in Karate in 2020 – Ivet Goranova.

In 2023 he launched his book "More! - Become More - Give More" which has defined his unique philosophy. Moses is an original. His insights come from his life journey and from the strong foundations he gained from his upbringing.

This book on Gratitude is a companion and workbook to MORE! and they should be used together.

Moses with Olympic Gold Medallist Ivet Goranova

What people are saying

Firstly, a massive congratulations to Moses Nalocca for this amazing masterpiece.

As founder of the Professional Speakers Academy, my passion is teaching talented business owners how to craft a presentation that impacts, inspires and makes income through the acquisition of new clients.

It is rare to find a coach with a powerful skill set and a proven success record of helping people to win whether that be winning in life, business or an Olympic medal.

When I first met Moses, immediately recognized a coach with the ability to inspire and motivate others in a lasting way.

He is a natural communicator on stage and full of energy.

Andy Harrington - Sunday Times Best Selling.Author of Passion Into Profit.

As a busy entrepreneur, I have been blessed to work with Moses, helping him go from a post-Covid 87kg, feeling lethargic, with brain fog and lacking the body that he once had, to reliving whom he is, regaining his amazing confidence and energy, looking fabulously congruent in his crusade to awaken others to the power they have to live, lead and love an even better life. Because sometimes you need to put yourself first to have an even greater positive impact in the world, to be selfish in order to be selfless.

If you believe that you want to have a positive effect in the lives of others, then I recommend that you read More! for a practical example of what it takes and where it can take you.

MARTIN SHARP
Multi-Award Winning International Consultant, Coach, Speaker and Author

"I have had the pleasure of coaching Moses for quite a few years. I first met him when he attended a workshop I was running. Two things immediately struck me at that first meeting - his energy and his presence. He is a phenomenal human being. He has an incredible appetite to grow, so that he can serve others even more.

It is an absolute privilege to work with this man. He has the biggest heart and I would recommend that anyone should interact with either his speaking or coaching. Ideally both!" -

Rich Waterman   - High Performance Coach

Dedication

I dedicate this book to my brother John Mark Nalocca and I am deeply grateful for the person he has become. I remember the day when we went to do athletics together and I introduced him to the sport for the first time. He was nine and I was fifteen. He immediately fell in love with athletics and went on to become a national champion in Italy and internationally. His level of commitment and excellence has been an inspiration and I am really proud of him. I am also deeply grateful for the most wonderful gift he could ever give me, a small, little young man who lovely calls me Uncle Moses.. I dedicate this book to him.

Published by
Authoritize Ltd
14, Croydon Road, Beddington,
Croydon, Surrey CR0 4PA
www.authoritize.co.uk
+44 (0)20 8688 2598

More Gratitude - Less Stress by Moses Nalocca
© 2023 Moses Nalocca
ISBN 978-1-915465-27-6 Paperback

Edited by Chris Day
Cover Design Ian Henderson
ian@2-h.co.uk

All rights reserved
The right to be reconised as the author of this work
has been asserted by Moses Nalocca in accordance
with the Designs and Copyright Act 1988 Section 77

No portion of this work may be copied in any way without the
prior written permission of the publishers

Table of Contents

Foreword - Veronica Tan	13
Preface - Chris Rowell	15
A word from Ivet Goranova	19
What does Gratitude really mean?	21
Getting the most out of this book	23
Introduction	27
Taking stock	35
Challenges	39

Gratitude Topics

1. Purpose	43
2. You are special!	61
3. Mothers	65
4. Children	71
5. Gratitude Reflection Exercise	77
6. Friendship	83
7. Random acts of Kindness	91
8. Surprises!	99
9. The Lift is broken	103
10. Wisdom	107
11. What are you attracting?	109

12. The Habit of Gratitude — 121

13. The Danger of Psudo-Gratitude — 179

14. Seize the Moment! — 131

15. Grateful for fear — 125

16. Being in the game — 137

17. Someone's opinion — 139

18. Attitude of gratitude builds confidence — 127

19. Gratitude first and last — 143

20. Radiating Gratitude — 151

> A dream you dream alone
> is only a dream.
> A dream you dream
> together is reality.
>
> Yoko Ono

FOREWORD

Veronica Tan

In 1992, along with my husband Richard Tan, we founded Success Resources (SR) which has become the world's largest education seminar company. Annually we host and produce 500+ entrepreneurial events across 37 countries including Australia, New Zealand, Singapore, Malaysia, South Africa, USA, Europe, Middle East, South America, and the UK. SR will empower 350,000+ entrepreneurs this year alone and have impacted 12 million people over its history. The recognised value of Success Resources' events is bringing about an exponential growth in global demand.

Today, our headline speakers include Tony Robbins, Sir Richard Branson, Robert Kiyosaki, Tom Brady, Lord Alan Sugar, Bill Clinton, Tony Blair. Sara Blakely, WILL.l.AM, Gary Vaynerchuck, Daymond John, and Pitbull Armando Christian Pérez, to name but a few.

Moses Nalocca

Moses is one of our many success stories. He was a seeker of inspiration and personal development and stretched hard to make it possible to attend one of our UPW (Unleash the Power Within) events with Tony Robbins which had a profound impact on him. So much so that he came back the following year as a Team Leader in our Meet and Greet team. Following that he joined the SR head office team and became a part of our preview events around the world.

Moses has flourished as an author, a high-level coach and a powerful speaker in his own right. I am delighted to have the opportunity of recognising him in his new book on Gratitude. It is a thought-provoking book and reminds us never to take anything for granted. I congratulate him on all of his achievements!

Chris Rowell

Firstly, I am grateful to Moses for the opportunity to write this Preface – Thank you buddy.

It's the 3rd of January 2021, the skies are blue, the sun is shining but there is a bit of snow on the ground and me and my amazing girlfriend Becka, are wrapped up with scarfs and hats. After a lovely pub lunch, we are walking our new puppy, Bruce through Etherow Country Park in Romiley, Stockport.

The day was like many other Sundays, and after settling down together for tea (it's what us Northerners call Dinner), it couldn't have ended more differently...

Without any warning at all, I had a sudden and severe Heart Attack! The first I knew of it was 3 days later when I woke up in hospital from a coma and I was immediately handed a phone to speak to Becka who told me that I had had a heart attack...

For me, I just woke up in hospital being cared for by some of the most amazing humans on the planet, however for Becka, this had been possibly the most traumatic experience that anyone could expect to go through. I had gone to the toilet before bed while Becka was in the Kitchen. I collapsed and dropped my mobile phone on the floor which she heard and instinctively knew something wasn't right.

After calling 999 she began CPR but quickly thought that she needed help, so she called our amazing neighbours and friends, Rob and Rebecca who immediately came to the house and Rebecca took over the CPR effectively keeping me alive! while Rob was comforting Becka. I was so fortunate that she wasn't working that evening, as Rebecca is a highly qualified Nurse who works in the Accident and Emergency department so I couldn't have had anyone better to perform CPR.

It took almost 20 minutes for the ambulance to arrive, so that immediate reaction from Becka and of course the 15+ minutes of intense CPR from Rebecca undoubtedly saved my life! (sometime later Rebecca commented that she was surprised she hadn't broken any ribs, such was the force needed to sustain my life)

To say that I am Grateful is perhaps one of the biggest understatements I have ever made, however without all these amazing Humans – not only would I not be here, but neither would my baby son Hugo, who was born some 18 months later! I am proud to say that I have become a father again for the 3rd time at the age of 51.

Additionally, my Girlfriend will soon become my wife after I proposed to her just a few months after my heart attack.
Every day I give gratitude for even the small things, and for every day-out, every sunset, every birthday and Christmas and every event that remains a memory I give gratitude. Even when faced with challenges etc, I am grateful to have those challenges. I know that I have so much more to give to I am Grateful for every single day.

> He who has health,
> has hope;
> and he who
> has hope,
> has everything.
>
> Thomas Carlyle

A gift for you!

I've realized in my life, that most of the times we are, we are blocked, our vision is obscured and closed by the limiting possibilities. Meanwhile, on the other side, we've got plenty of things in the past, in the present and in the future to look at. And one of the best practical tools I can give you right now is my guided meditation, where I will take you through Three Steps of Gratitude.

I know for sure that you have wealth inside of you, you've got emotional wealth, you've got physical wealth, you've got memories wealth, so you are already wealthy. This tool I am gifting you will help you to understand this on an even deeper level.

Just scan to get your free gift. Enjoy!

Ivet Goranova

I know very well that when you compete in any sport at an elite level, any success you enjoy is not just down to you, but it is a result of the support team around you. This has taught me much about the importance of Gratitude. I am immensely grateful for the skills and qualities that the universe has blessed me with and also the opportunities I have been give to put those skills to good use. I have learnt to take nothing for granted. Everything is a gift.

My sport is Karate and this has opened many doors for me. I have competed international in Paris, Belarus, Paris, Tokyo, the USA and Dubai and have become a multiple Gold Medallist.

With my Mindset Coach Moses, to guide me, he has helped me to develop a deep attitude of gratitude for all the many wonderful people, opportunities, and places that life has brought me.

For me, Gratitude is the feeling of empathising and realising the value of what has been received. To give thanks is to complete an energy exchange, whether it is with yourself or with another.

Awareness of gratitude helps me to love more, to support, to motivate both myself and others. Gratitude is not expected, gratitude is given!

As athletes, we are used to everyone working for us and sometimes we don't appreciate what we get to succeed. We must be able to be grateful to ourselves, no matter if we are at the top or not, to be grateful to the people who help us, to be grateful to the universe for what we receive and to enjoy the little things in life!

> Give yourself a gift of five minutes of contemplation in awe of everything you see around you. Go outside and turn your attention to the many miracles around you. This five-minute-a-day regimen of appreciation and gratitude will help you to focus your life in awe.
>
> Wayne Dyer

What does Gratitude really mean?

I love to look at words and to break them down into separate syllables. For me, the word Gratitude naturally breaks down into GRA and TITUDE. I see that as 'Grace' and 'Attitude' or an attitude of grace. So what is grace? Grace is a gift from God. Grace is given. You don't earn it, and you don't buy it. Grace is a gift and the biggest gift that we've been given of grace, is life itself.

Attitude is the filter with which we look at life, and all of the graces we have received. A positive attitude helps us to see clearly the value of those graces. A negative attitude blinds us to those graces and dishonours those gifts we have been given.

When you are angry, you are dishonouring that gift, when you are anxious, you are dishonouring that gift. When you have hatred, and you're not able to forgive, you are dishonouring the gift of life that has been given to you. Even when you wake up each morning with an abundance of grace available to you, you are turning away and rejecting it. How can you ever expect to achieve your full potential on your own?
To put it simply, Gratitude is a special quality which puts us in resonance with the universe and attracts good things into our lives.

We learned about gratitude
and humility - that so many people
had a hand in our success,
from the teachers who inspired us
to the janitors who kept our school
clean... and we were taught to value
everyone's contribution and treat
everyone with respect.

Michelle Obama

Getting the most out of this book

Some books are beautiful works of art destined to spend their lives sitting on a coffee table, trying to impress visitors. They get dusted from time to time, but are never read. They are for show, rather than enlightenment. This is not one of those books.

For this book to fulfill its purpose, you need to break a cardinal rule and **write** in it. I realise that this goes against everthing we have ever been taught by parents, teachers and especially, librarians!

As the author of this work, I hereby give you express **permission** to break the rules and **write** in this book. In fact, if you don't write in it, it will not fulfil its purpose in life - and neither will you!

This book is designed to draw out ideas from your brain that have not seen the light of day for some time. I have written it with the purpose of delving deep into your brain, and waking up long lost thoughts, dreams and desires that may be gathering dust. Having done so, they will only help you if you then write them down immediately on the pages provided for the purpose. Nobody but you will ever see them, so don't be constrained or shy! It is only by writing them down that they will come alive and serve you.

We have so much locked up in our brains that gets pushed to one side by the torrent of irrelevance that we permit to enter through our ears and eyes. Much of it isn't worthy of the space and obscures the important stuff that we urgently need to guide us through the challenges ahead. If only we had a system cleaner to defrag our brains whilst we sleep! That is why this book is so important.

When you wake up a dormant thought, it is a fragile thing and can be forgotten almost as fast as it came to us. You need to spike it with a pencil and pin it down on a page, so that it can't vanish.

Thoughts have a very good habit of joining hands and turning into ideas. Enough ideas can trigger action, and action causes results to happen. It all starts with a flimsy and fragile thoughtlet, that was given the chance to live and breathe by being captured on paper.

Do use a pencil rather than a pen as this gives you the opportunity to use an eraser and to shuffle your thoughts, order them and smarten them up. If you allow the words in this book to sink in, and you are ready to capture the thoughts that they generate, who is to know what powerful concepts might emerge. It is up to you!

Capturing your thoughts and insights

Throughout this book you will find blank pages. They are there for you to use to recall the thoughts that may be triggered from the chapter you are reading.

In the future, it will be these pages you will be reading, rather than the text of the book. It is here that you will be reminded of the nuggets of gold that came to you from your insights. You have all the answers you need inside your head. Write them down!

In addition, I have scattered some Gratitude Journal pages across the book. Whilst these pages are duplicated, the thing that will have changed is you. You will find that you have difference insights as you progress through the book. As a result, the information you capture on these pages will reflect this evolution.

Moses Nalocca

Introduction

Do you believe in miracles?

It was the Jackson Sisters in 1976 who recorded the song "I believe in Miracles" although it was actually written way back in 1948

*I believe in miracles, baby
I believe in you!*

My coach, Rich Waterman once said to me, "Miracles happen every day, and every day they come your way." So this became my mantra. Every time I said this to myself, it made me look out for Blessings in everything that was happening around me. I soon discovered that I didn't ever need to look very far. Blessings were always running towards me. I believe that the world is full of blessings and the universe is there to bless us. But not everybody thinks this way.

Because I am a naturally positive person, I have become very aware of negative people and negative things happening around me. Negative people are the ones who believe in conspiracy theories. They know the price of everything and the value of nothing. They are the ones that have pity parties in the pub where they share stories of how unfair the world has been to them. Nothing pleases them more than to burst positive person's bubble. For them, it's a result!

The trouble is that, with so many negative things happening around us, and on the news, it is difficult to prove them wrong. They shout the loudest, and they are buying the next round! **However, you can see what they cannot.**

You can see all the micro blessings that we all too easily take for granted. Such as the gift of;

- A new day full of possibilities. What we make of them is down to us.
- A warm and comfortable place to live. Of the 8 billion people in the world, there are only 2.5 billions homes for them.
- A cold glass of milk from the fridge to start your day. Over two billion people in the world do not have any refrigeration. Most of them live in the hottest of climates
- A toilet in your home. 4.5 billion people do not have a toilet in their home. Surely this is a fundamental right?
- Food on your table to feed your family. **In the UK alone, 26,082 TONES of food is thrown away everyday.** Yet there are people who cannot afford food.

Never take any the gifts you have for granted. Be grateful every day.

In your own experience, you already know that far more good has come your way, than the reverse.

You already know the many ways that the universe smiles at you every day. Abundance is all around us, even if the riches we may currently posess have not yet manifested themselves as money. There are many other currencies where we are already millionaires. Money will follow when we are ready to use it wisely. Not before!

Take a moment to look around you. Filter out all those things that you can't control or have no influence over. Focus only on those things which directly affect you and are in your circle of influence. This simplifies things, and takes away that feeling of helplessness we have about all those worrying things happening around the world.

With this new focus, you can see clearly all those many good things around you and the miracles that are happening right now. **Be grateful! Now write them down....**

> Everyone has a purpose in life
> and a unique talent to give to others.
> When we blend this unique talent with
> service to others,
> we experience the ecstasy
> and exultation of our34 spirit,
> which is the ultimate goal of all goals.
>
> Kallam Anji Reddy

MORE Gratitude Less Stress

MORE Gratitude Less Stress

Taking Stock

Before we get too far into the book, it would be valuable to take stock and remind ourselves of all the many blessings we have. Now, this is not ignoring all the challenges we have in our lives. It is not ignoring the fact that we are not currently where we are supposed to be, or deserve to be. Reminding ourselves of our many Blessings is to remind us of the tools, qualities, experiences, and insights we have been given to get ourselves to where we need to be.

On the basis that the feintest of ink is better than the strongest of memory, use the space on the next page to list all the gifts you have been given. These gifts are the foundations of your future.

- Your qualities
- Your attitude to life
- The skills you have
- The people that are around you
- The lessons that life has taught you
- The qualifications you have
- Your ambitions
- Your energy and motivation

Take stock of all the assets you have for your journey ahead. Spend some time right now, and focus on the special person you are.

Which of your many gifts are you most grateful for?

MORE Gratitude Less Stress

Moses Nalocca

Challenges

It doesn't matter what you are facing or what fears you might have for the future. With the Universe looking after your back, no matter what challenges you may believe are ahead of you, you will be given the strength to conquer them – so be strong.

You see, as human beings, we are either coming out of a terrible situation, or we are in a terrible situation, or we are heading towards one. Life is there to teach us, but it also gives us the skills we need to get through it and to succeed. **Take care of yourself – you are special!**

Now this is a time for honesty. As you take stock of your assets, it may well be that there are some talents that you have forgotten about. Over the course of our lives we have been many different people and have done various jobs or even careers in the past. What were the specific skills you developed back then? As we move on to new careers, it is easy to forget what we used to be good at, and what people asked our advice for. These are still assets that you have which could be repurposed in the future. Who knows when we might need them again?

As you list all of your qualities, talents, skills, qualifications, go right back so that nothing is missed. Who knows, you might get the inspiration for a new direction or even a new career.?

What advice would you give to your younger self right now?

FUTURE SELF

What is going to be different with your future self?

What will you change?

What will you never do again?

Who will be on your journey?

Learned	Enjoy	Grateful

FUTURE SELF

Date: ....

Notes

Purpose

I believe that we are all divided into two groups. There are those who understand what their purpose is, and are striving to achieve it. Then there are those who have not yet gained clarity on what their purpose and direction is, in their life, and are striving to discover what it is.

Having clarity of purpose is one of the foundations for having a satisfying life. Without it, nothing makes sense. It is like having the best car in the world, but no petrol to start the engine.

Some people discover their purpose at an early age and are able to focus on it and prepare for it whilst they are still a child. Having a purpose gives you focus.

There is nothing sadder to see people in later life who have nothing to get up for, and whose only purpose is to survive, day by day.

We spend our lives learning something new every day. We develop new skills and have new experiences. What difference would it have made to you if, when you started your current career, you knew what you know now? How many people are in that same position at the moment where your knowledge could be invaluable to them? These days it is easier than ever to turn your knowledge into a business online. There is no reason why anybody should be without a purpose. You have valuable knowledge that people will pay for.

Moses Nalocca

Describe what you believe your purpose is in life

MORE Gratitude Less Stress

Moses Nalocca

MORE Gratitude Less Stress

GRATITUDE LOG

DATE :

- _____
- _____
- _____

DATE :

- _____
- _____
- _____

DATE :

- _____
- _____
- _____

DATE :

- _____
- _____
- _____

DATE :

- _____
- _____
- _____

Finding Answers

We all need to discover the answers to those deep questions within us. Why am I here? What does the universe want of me? How can I repay the universe for all the many blessings and talents it has showered on me? A life focused just on self and without contribution is a sad and meaningless life.

If you have yet to discover what your true purpose in life is, don't worry. The universe is leaving you clues all the time.

Happiness cannot be travelled to, owned, earned, worn or consumed. Happiness is the spiritual experience of living every minute with love, grace, and gratitude.

Denis Waitley

Moses Nalocca

What is your true purpose?

What is stopping your from achieving your purpose?

Date: ....

Notes

What Blessings do you already have that can help you achieve your Purpose?

Have you discovered what your true purpose is in life? The things you are most grateful for will give you a clue.

A teenager was being interviewed by a career guidance teacher. "What do you want to do when you leave school?" The teacher asked. "Dunno Miss" The pupil answered. "Alright, I know that you don't know what you want to do, but if you did, what would that be?" "I want to be a chef" came the answer. Hidden inside us all are the answers to all the questions we have. Sometimes, all it takes is for someone to ask the right question.

We all have the potential of leaving a meaningful legacy to the world when we eventually pass away. Ask yourself, what will people say of me at my funeral? I know it is not a pleasant thought, but it does focus the mind. Whatever it is that you want to be remembered for, it is never too late to start. There is no greater motivator than to realise that life is slipping away in front of us.

The saying, 'Life is too short' is very true. Life is not a rehearsal. We only get one chance at it. Don't waste that chance.

For me as a speaker, my purpose is very clear. I want to touch as many people as possible and plant seeds in their mind that will blossom and grow in the years ahead. When I eventually die, I will have the satisfaction of knowing that my thoughts, ideas and inspirations will live on in the lives of those I have trained or coached.

If you have not yet gained clarity on your big purpose in life, now is the time to discover what it is, and what the universe has been trying to tell you all of this time. It is time to take out your white ear pods, and enjoy the silence for long enough to think. Switch off the noise of life, and allow your creative thoughts to flow. Your greatest insights will come in moments like these.

As you open yourself to the universe you can be certain that the answers you have been looking for were there all the time.

Looking back at my life, I have been many different people at different times and have had many different jobs. I knew that, when I worked on the beach setting up the sunbeds, picking up the rubbish and raking the sand, that I would not be doing this for the rest of my life.

But I also knew that if my section of the beach was the cleanest and that I provided a cheerful and professional service, then I would do well. I worked with joy, knowing that I would be making money. I know my clients would come and discover this was the best beach in the world. This allowed me to step into my purpose.

No matter how menial a job is, if you make the most of it, other opportunities will grow out of it. This has been my experience throughout my career. Every time we do our best in one field, the universe unblocks something else. And when the universe unblocks something else, we can step up to another new dimension.

The more you grow, the more you enter into another level of purpose.

Right now, one of my purposes is to inspire you, with this book, with my other books with my programs. That's my focus and I am putting 100% of my purpose on it right now.

It is worth remembering that some of the influence you have by just doing your day-to-day activities, will be lost on you. Something you said in a conversation was heard and picked up by a stranger and it fell on fertile soil. By living your purpose and being the best version of yourself that you can be, the ripples you leave in the pond can travel a long way after an event.

Sometimes, years later, somebody will come up to you and thank you for something you said to them at the time, which made a difference to their lives. You may have forgotten, but they didn't!

Remember, you are always 'on-stage". You cannot step away from your purpose and be a lesser person. It disrespects the universe.

Be in your strength.
Be in your passion.
Be in your purpose.

What qualities, skills, talents and experiences make you unique? Don't be shy! You need to know where you make the most contribution.

MORE Gratitude Less Stress

Moses Nalocca

You are special!

I believe that none of us is an accident, and all of us are exactly where we are meant to be, right now. We have a role and a purpose, even though that might not yet be clear to us. This book is a tool to help you find out what your purpose is by helping you look at life around you, in a completely new way. It will also show you how unique you are.

Few people realise that one of the building blocks of us all is Carbon. Whilst we hear a lot about it these days, it was not a natural substance that was originally a part of the earth. Carbon arrived on earth from meteorites and asteroids. So the carbon inside everyone of us is from the explosion of a star. We are made of Star Dust. It is in our DNA. Not only that, but there was a billion-to-one chance that we wouldn't make it. That's the number of seeds that were in competition to bring you into the world. But you made it, and were born as a champion! To have made it so far, you are a winner – and a Star!

In this book, I want you to focus on your uniqueness. It is this that will determine your future. You were born on purpose, for a purpose. You were not a mistake, you are not an accident. There are no coincidences in the universe. You need to celebrate who you are and be massively grateful. This book will help you to do that.here are two types of people on this earth, those who take, and those who give. Which are you?

It doesn't matter how much you accumulate in this life; the cars; the houses; the bling and the gizmos, you can't take them with you when you inevitably leave the planet.

So let's not focus on what we can get. Let's focus on what we can become in order to give more.

> God's gift to us is life.
> Our gift to him is
> what we do with it

MORE Gratitude Less Stress

Mothers

FIRST MY MOTHER FOREVER MY FRIEND

O f all the people who have come into our lives, our parents are the most special. In our formative years they are giving us their love and affection in so many ways. A mother's love is unconditional and creates a deep bond that will stay with us throughout our lives.

Mothers are the only people who truly have our best interest at heart. They care enough to correct us when we are going off track.

They teach us our values, give us discipline and help us to be the best version of ourselves.

As we bring friends into our lives, it is our mothers who see things in them that we might not see, although this might be painful for us at the time.

It is our mothers who introduce us to spiritual values, and the word of the Lord. A mother's biggest duty is to equip us with values and knowledge we will need to to grow and thrive. We don't always appreciate them at the time or realise that they do have our best interests at heart.

Growing up, many teenagers resent their mother's influence over them and yearn to discover the world on their own, without fully understanding the dangers that are outside the front door.

There is a saying "Employ a teenager whilst they still know it all!"

There are times in all our lives when we forget how much our parents sacrificed to bring us into the world, and to help us grow and develop.

When we are headstrong, aggressive, rude and uncaring towards them, we hurt them far deeper that we could ever realise. The worse pain is a parent's pain. We should never forget it.

If anyone deserved our deepest gratitude, it is them..

Never miss an opportunity to show it.

It is easier to build strong children than to repair broken men.

Frederick Douglass

What are you most grateful to your mother for?

How can you show more Gratitude to your parents?

MORE Gratitude Less Stress

GRATITUDE JOURNAL

DATE _____

S M T W T F S

TODAY I AM GRATEFUL FOR

TODAY'S TOP 3 INTENTIONS

DAILY WATER TRACKER

DAILY FOOD TRACKER

WHAT I AM LEARNING

I LIKE ABOUT MYSELF

NOTES

> Children begin by
> loving their parents;
> after a time
> they judge them;
> rarely, if ever,
> do they forgive them.
>
> Oscar Wilde

Write down an "AHA!" moment when an idea came to you

Children

My first experience of working with children was as a coach when I was 14. I was asked to help with the children's Sunday School group in the church where my mum was the Pastor. It was a wonderful experience. I involved them with music and was able to practice my speaking, coaching and storytelling skills. Working with children is more rewarding than anything else.

Children are such a precious gift. Their minds are like a sponge and are keen to soak up every little gem of knowledge. As adults, our job is not to direct, but to inspire. We should never impose our thinking on them, but nurture their enquiring minds and let them make the connections for themselves. You are their steward, not their manager, and beware, they remember everything! Especially the things you don't want them to!

Make having a family, the biggest choice you can make. It is a commitment for life and also one of the greatest joys you can have.

If you have children, you will already know the multitude of things you are grateful for. All of those life milestones as they grow up; being there with them as they discover and appreciate new things; the friendships they make; their achievements and successes they enjoy.

What were you most grateful for when growing up as a child?

Life is never boring when you have children. They are always a source if wonderment and joy. As they grow up, they will be a source of constant surprise and delight.
There is a lyric from the film "The King and I", where Ana is teaching the King's children.

"It's a very ancient saying,
But a true and honest thought,
That if you become a teacher,
By your pupils you'll be taught."

Both as a parent and also as a teacher, you cannot fail to get a new perspective on things when viewed through a child's eyes.

Children will not remember how many cars, how many houses, how much money you they had. Children will remember all those wonderful experiences you gave them.

> Live so that when your children think of fairness, caring, and integrity, they think of you.
>
> H. Jackson Brown, Jr.

Counting your Blessings
What Blessings do our children give us?

MORE Gratitude Less Stress

Moses Nalocca

Gratitude Reflection Exercise

For you to gain the most from this practical exercise, I must ask you not to read on and to skim through the words. It will not help you, and it will spoil it for when you are ready to do it properly. This is a powerful process and will require you to find a quiet space and plan to avoid any interruptions. You will get the most out of it, if you keep your eyes closed, and your mind open.

To start

Take a deep breath and slow down your brain

Your brain is bursting with things to tell you and remind you about. You need to put all of that on hold and just empty your mind

Filter out any background noise

Take another deep breath and sit straight

Make sure your legs and arms are not crossed. Put the palms of your hands on your legs and keep them there.

And take another deep breath.

And as you take another deep breath, I want you to think of a moment in the childhood, a memory that is so far away. It doesn't have to be big or small, it just has to be a memory.

Go drag it into your current memory. And get this memory of your special moment from your childhood, like when your dad taught you to ride the bike, or when your grandfather bought you an ice cream, or when you had your first bicycle.
Or when you went for your first day at primary school. When you fell in love with your first girlfriend in elementary school.

Grab that memory. And right now I want you to stretch in front of you your right hand and grab that memory.

Hold it in your hands. Breathe it, feel it, get back to that moment.

And as you get to that moment and you hold it in your hand, put a big smile on your face. Because you're deeply grateful for it. smile and say thank you.

And a count of three. Bring your right hand on your heart. 321. Go and stay now you've got one memory to be grateful. And get there stay there.
Breathe it, stay in that moment.

Stay in that present moment, be there.

What's can you feel?
What are you seeing?
What are you smelling?
What are you hearing?

Stay there in that beautiful memory of gratitude from your childhood that you're carrying with you in your heart right now.

Now take another deep breath.

Now I want you to think of a moment of love.
Whether it's love as a moment of passion,
or whether it's love with somebody giving you a cuddle or caress, a moment of love,
where you're hugging your children,
or you're hugging your father, your mother.

Think about another moment of love. And as you stretch your left hand, I want you to grab that memory.

Hold it tight.
Breathe it.
Hold it in your hands.
And as your right hand is in your heart,
your left hand is grabbing that moment feeling it, seeing it, touching it.
And now the count of three.
bring your left hand on your heart. Three, two, one. Go.

Now you have two magic moments in your heart.
Hold them there breathe it.

Now you've got two amazing memories, a moment of love, a moment of passion.

A moment of understanding.
Hold it there.
Stay there.
Breathe it, feel it.

You've now got two moments, so put a big smile on your face and say thank you. Thank you. Thank you.

Now take a deep breath.

And I want you to raise your hands in the
air in a sign of victory. Both hands.
As a champion winning that gold medal.
I want you to find a memory that you are proud of.
Something that you have achieved,
something that you have done.
And you tell yourself, bravo!
Well done! Congratulations! You did it!

Hold on to that moment and relive that memory

Now take a deep breath.

and relax.

Thank you.

MORE Gratitude Less Stress

What are the most important things you have learned from children, both yours, and other people's?

Friendship

Life is partly what we make it, and partly what it is made by the friends we choose.

Tennessee Williams

True friendship is very special and can last for a lifetime. Some people may be with us for a reason, others for a season, but if a friendship is genuine, it can and should be there for life. The truth is that we have forgotten what Friendship actually means.

A friend is not a person who happens to be on Facebook and who clicked the 'Friend' button. Nor is it a 'Like' on Instagram. Nor is it somebody you once had a zoom call with.

A true friend is someone you actually know and have shared time with. Someone with whom you have had sufficient time to bond with and to learn about their qualities and values.

A true friend is somebody with shared values and who you can call or visit out of the blue, and would be welcomed in.

A friend is somebody you can be speaking to, and then not see for a year. When you meet again, continue the conversation where you left it.

True friendship multiplies the good
in life and divides its evils.
Strive to have friends,
for life without friends is like
life on a desert island...
to find one real friend in a lifetime
is good fortune;
to keep him is a blessing.

Baltasar Gracian

None of us have any choice of who our family are. They are who they are, whether we like it or not. Everybody's family contains both the good, the bad and the ugly within the in-laws and the out-laws. But we can choose our friends, and we should do so with care. They will become our support team for life and those who we can really rely on.

Our three peer groups

We need to have three peer groups around us. The first is the group that we **lead**. These are people that we inspire, we guide, we lead, we teach. These are people we are giving out to and they are getting from us.

The second category are the people that we **laugh with**. These are people who are playing the same game as us but on a similar level. We can relax with them. We don't need to show off, teach or learn from them. We just have time to relax, and tend to not engage in anything heavy. We just chill out, laugh and have fun.

The final category is the people that we **look up to** and learn from. These are the people who are playing the game at a higher level than us. People who have more knowledge and experience than ourselves and are prepared to share it. We look at them we aspire to be like them and achieve the same results.

We probably have a healthy mix of all three types of people in our circle.

This group of people are your most valuable and you should never take them for granted. Some you may not see from months at a time, other you may see every week . Never take thees friends for granted.

Spend some time right now acknowledging these friends. Those people who have been by your side through all your challenges, great and small. Through break-ups or even a divorce. They have been by your side when you had nothing and nobody.

True friends are for life, whether we see them regularly or not, they are an essential part of our journey. Be grateful!

*I cannot even imagine where
I would be today were it not for
that handful of friends
who have given me
a heart full of joy.
Let's face it, friends
make life a lot more fun.*

Charles R. Swindoll

Gratitude for friendship

MORE Gratitude Less Stress

GRATITUDE JOURNAL

DATE

TODAY I AM GRATEFUL FOR

MY TODAY'S BEST PLAN

WHAT I AM LEARNING

NOTES

I LIKE ABOUT MYSELF

Random Acts of Kindness

As kids growing up, we become used to random surprises happening all the time. It is part of the joy of being a child. An unexpected day out by the sea. Cakes for tea. Ice cream on a hot day. A visit to the cinema. All little things in themselves, but all of them are memories we can revisit with gratitude. In many instances, it was not the size of the occasion or the gift, that made it special, it was just a moment when somebody demonstrated that for us they cared or loved us by giving us a nice surprise.

Although these experiences may be well in the past, the lessons they taught us are very relevant today. Spreading a little joy can go a long way in making life a little nicer both for ourselves, and the people we meet.

In our busy and stressful lives, we can get so wound up in our troubles and challenges, that we can forget about those around us. As part of my gratitude journey, I have discovered that a tiny moment making someone I meet feel special, makes me feel special as well. A random act of kindness.

When I was unclear about what the universe wanted of me, and I was between opportunities, I would default to working in a bar or a restaurant. Because of my energy and enthusiasm, I found this to be a positive experience and I made sure it was the same for my customers. But it wasn't all a one-way street. Some customers went out of their way to find out my name – and to use it throughout the evening. We all appreciate it when people use our names.

Remember all of those random and unexpected moments of kindness and appreciation you have received and have been grateful for.

It makes us feel special. I certainly felt motivated to look after them during their visit.

Initially when you are providing service in a bar or restaurant, the relationship with your customer is a normal customer / servant relationship. However, if you show them kindness, this breaks that mould and immediately builds rapport. Rapport is what tips are made of!

Every time I go to a restaurant, the first thing I ask the waiter is, "What's your name? Where are you from?" I am genuinely interested. If I am open, then I will learn something.

> They say that everybody has a story to tell. Make sure that yours is not a cautionary tale!

I believe in making the most of every time I meet someone new. After all, I believe that there are no coincidences, if the Universe has brought two people together, it has done so for a reason. It is my challenge to find out what that is.

It is the same when I am travelling in a taxi. I am always interested in the driver. After all, they are famous for their wisdom! They spend their day driving people who sit silently in the back of the car. What a waste of an opportunity! No matter who you meet, there is always something you can learn from them. All you need to do is to speak to them to find out what it is. Then listen.

What actions can you do to demonstrate to your circle of special friends that you are grateful and appreciate them?

I know that there are many lonely people out there. I have relatives who live alone, and who hardly speak to anyone during the day. You would be surprised how powerful a random smile or a cheery word can be. It can be the highlight of their day!

Make it an objective to speak to a stranger, or to make a random act of kindness to someone you have never met, I guarantee you will have a really great day yourself.

The next time you go for a coffee, pay extra so that the next person can have a free coffee. They won't know who it was from, but they will know that the Universe loves them.

When you do something like this, you will realise that you are really rich, both as a human being, and rich in your soul, because you are giving something to somebody, knowing that they can never repay you, or give you anything in exchange. That makes you feel good.

A random act of kindness could be helping a lady carry her shopping bags in a shop; or helping her climb onto a bus or the train. Maybe even giving them your seat. All random acts of kindness. All opportunities to feel good about yourself. So how good do you want to feel today? You know what to do!

Random acts of kindness you have experienced

Random acts of kindness you will perform

Each day holds a surprise.
But only if we expect it
can we see, hear, or feel it
when it comes to us.
Let's not be afraid to
receive each day's surprise,
whether it comes to us as sorrow
or as joy. It will open a
new place in our hearts,
a place where we can welcome
new friends and celebrate
more fully our shared humanity.

Henri Nouwen

Surprises

A friend of mine became prosperous and decided that he wanted to so something special for his parents. Without their knowing, he purchased a new house for them as a surprise. He then paid for them to go on a special holiday. While they were away, he arranged for everything in their house to be packed up and moved to their new house. It took ages as there were 50 years of memories to be packaged and moved.

When his parents returned he took them to their new house. Much to his surprise, they were not happy. Although their original home was small by comparison, and in need of decoration, nevertheless, it was their home and they were happy there. It was full of all their family memories. This was where their children were born and grew up. But now it was all gone, and they weren't expecting it.

With surprises, do think them through. What might seem wonderful for us, might be seen in a completely different way by someone else. Be sensitive to the needs of others. We are all very different.

To receive a surprise, you need to be open for it and receptive. Not everyone is. Some people feel that they are undeserving and so shy away from those times when the universe is trying to reward them. No matter what it is that you are allowing to steal your sense of worth, you need to reframe your mindset and let the light back in.

There are so many pleasant surprises that happen to us every day, so focus on them. Do you know why? Because if you focus on those pleasant surprises, you are expanding those surprises.

Where focus goes, the energy flows. This is what Tony Robbins says all the time.

If we allow ourselves to focus on the surprises, those surprises will expand. Suddenly you find yourself surrounded by incredible surprises, from your friends, from your family, from your life, from your work. There are surprises to be found everywhere.

At the same time, you also need to focus on those around you. How can you bring a little sunlight into their lives? Don't let any day go past without finding ways to make people feel great about what they are doing.

Make it personal, make it genuine, make it unexpected, make it memorable.

There is no surprise more magical than the surprise of being loved: It is God's finger on man's shoulder.

Charles Morgan

What wonderful surprises have you had in your life that you remain grateful for?

Moses Nalocca

Who is it that makes the biggest difference in your life? What do you appreciate the most about them?

The Lift is broken. Take the Stairs

If you are serious about being the best you can be, you will have already discovered that there are no shortcuts. Success might be on the 10th floor, but if you seriously want it, you need to take the stairs, not the lift. Each step has something to teach us. If we try to leap up the stairs, two at a time, we will miss some important lessons. There are no prizes for rushing, just for successfully putting your learning into action. **Speed is the enemy of quality. Aways hurry slowly!**

> He who knows ALL THE **ANSWERS** HAS NOT BEEN ASKED ALL THE **QUESTIONS**
>
> — CONFUCIUS

MORE Gratitude Less Stress

Moses Nalocca

Wisdom

It is amazing how much common sense came out of the mouth of the Chinese philosopher, Confucius, born 2574 years ago! The fact that this wisdom has lasted, and is still being talked about today, tells us that he is worth listening to. On the subject of Wisdom, Confucius said:

There are three methods by which we may learn wisdom:

- First, by reflection, which is the noblest;
- Second, by imitation, which is the easiest;
- and third, by experience, which is the bitterest.

Unless you make a conscious decision to separate yourself from the noise of the day on a regular basis, and make time in your schedule for quietness, you will never hear that inner voice which is shouting at you in order to gain your attention.

It has been said that we have inside us all of the answers we need for every confusing situation. All we lack are the questions in order to access it.

An experienced business person was once asked what he thought about a particular situation. He replied, "Don't ask me what I think until I have heard what I am going to say." Sometimes we need to dig down deep into our minds to find answers through talking.

A really good way to do this is by answering a question. The brain will start working on the answer immediately and you may be surprised by what it comes up with. Because it comes from deep in your memory, it may well be something you hadn't initially thought about. "Don't ask me what I think till I have heard what I am going to say." Profound.

Wisdom is the ability to remain silent while you are considering a question and only speak once your brain have formutated the answer. Most people talk before they think, not after.

Wisdom is also the quality of feeding your brain with wise words of others. There isn't enough time for you to think everything through yourself. Let others do some of the grunt work.

> Experience is not what happens to you; it's what you do with what happens to you.
>
> Aldous Huxley

What questions do you need to ask yourself, in order to get the answers you need?

You cannot control what happens to you, but you can control your attitude toward what happens to you, and in that, you will be mastering change rather than allowing it to master you.

Brian Tracy

What are you attracting into your Life?

The simple answer is that we attract into our lives, that which we think about the most. Be it good or bad.

Some people live fearful lives and focus on all the threats and dangers that they believe surround them every day. Bad news consumes them. Their mantra is "What if?" and they apply it to everything around them but there is an antidote.

If, instead of thinking what could happen, you focused on all the many things you are grateful for? Would you feel better or worse?

Filling our minds with positive things will not make bad things go away, but it will help to put them into perspective and make them less important.

If you want to attract better things into your life, be a better person. Avoid talking about negative things, and avoid people who see the worse in every situation.

The people surrounding you are a reflection of who you really are. The way they talk will give you a clue. If you don't like what you hear, maybe you are surrounded by the wrong people.

Looking back, how grateful are you for the many 'Lucky Escapes' you had when you realised that some opportunities were not for you - and you were proved right!

When did you last see the film "The Secret"? Seeing it once is not enough. The messages are so profound that you need to be reminded of them regularly.

I  want you to focus on all the opportunities that you may be able to attract because of the person you have become, or are becoming.

All the opportunities are out there but most of the time we are not aware of them. Our brain looks the other way. There must be a reason for this.

Either our brain knows we are not ready for it yet, or because it would not be right for us, right now. Maybe later in our journey we would be ready. Never forget that the Universe always has our best interest in mind. That is not necessarily what we want ourselves.

You build on failure.
You use it as a stepping stone.
Close the door on the past.
You don't try to
forget the mistakes,
but you don't dwell on them either.
You don't let them have
any of your energy, or
any of your time,
or any of your space.

Johnny Cash

Looking back, I am grateful for those times when the Universe said "no" to someting that I really wanted. At the time it was right. Now I understand that. Sometimes what you want is not what you need.

You know what? Based on my experience, I've understood that life often gives you the lesson, and then explains it to you later on.

So, what I want you to do in this section, is to acknowledge all those opportunities as they arrive and evaluate them in a logical and unemotional way. Realise that not all of them will be right for you, and some might pose a danger. Look out for 'Shiny Pennies' that could distract you from your right path. If you are confused, seek the council of your inner circle of friends. That is what they are there for.

By working on yourself, you will attract even more into your life because that's what you deserve. Only you have the power to say 'yes' or 'no', if it is right for you or not.

I realised in my life that every single experience or job I had, was a stepping stone for me to build up my career.

Most of the time we look at a job as a necessity for the short term, and miss the fact that it might well be there to teach us something we need later, as move on the the next thing.

What jobs have you had that you are most grateful for? What did you learn or become as a result?

Let me tell you one thing, the universe will never give you anything that you cannot handle. In this section, I want you to be grateful for your work, even if it's cleaning the toilets. Be grateful for it.

I remember when I was a 16 years old, my job was to be the beach boy, putting all the sun beds and making sure the beach was tidied up. I was doing it with so much gratitude and so much joy because I was earning money. I was so enthusiastic, I wasn't grumbling and complaining about it. It was a summer job, and I was doing it for myself. I gave it 150% of my effort.

My enthusiasm and attutide were noticed and I was promoted, first of all to a waiter and later on, when I had proved myself again, to manager. For three seasons, I was managing people who were older than me. I was in charge of the orders, the reservations, and everything. All this simply because I gave each job my all.

What wisdom do you have now that you wish you had when you were growing up?

When I went in sales, I started going door to door selling utilities. I worked hard and ended up as team leader. I was promoted to supervisor and finally I managed three call centres with 600 people reporting to me. It all has to start somewhere.

With the job that you have now, it might not be the best, but if you work at it, it could take you anywhere.

Whatever the job, be grateful for the salary, be grateful for that opporunity and take nothing for granted.

I know that a job is just a job. It may not be what you really want. It may be that the Universe has given it to you because you are not yet ready for the one it has in mind for you.

If you are to climb life's ladder, it only works if you are prepared to give 150% to each opportunity. There are no prizes for just turning up.

Life will promote you when you deserve it and not before. Be honest with yourself, are you always complaining? Are you always grumbling? Are you late for work regularly? Are you putting the least amount effort into your hours at work, or the least amount of enthusiasm? If you're not putting sufficient energy into your current work, don't expect the universe to reward you with something else.

If you want things to change, you are the one that has to change first.

GRATITUDE JOURNAL

TODAY I AM GRATEFUL FOR

MY TODAY'S BEST PLAN

WHAT I AM LEARNING

NOTES

I LIKE ABOUT MYSELF

Have you ever taken a step back to look at how you behave at work and how others see you? Do you like what you see?

Are you always complaining and pointing the finger at others? Are you delegating your work to others and not doing your fair share?

Are you the type of person who supports your colleagues, and are excited for them and their success? Or are you envious of them? Are you worried that they will shine brighter than you?

Are you a team player? What sort of person do your work colleagues think you are? If you're a team player, the universe will notice and will reward you.

You see, being a team player is vital. Because this is one of the first foundations of leadership. If you respect the people you work with, they will respect you and they will look on you as their leader. Every leader needs to earn the respect of their team if they are to succeed.

Leadership is a mindset based of respect, care and shared goals.

Make it a habit to tell
people thank you.
To express your appreciation,
sincerely and without
the expectation of
receiving anything in return.
Truly appreciate those around you,
and you'll soon find many others around
you. Truly appreciate life, and you'll find
that you have more of it.

Ralph Marston

The Habit of Gratitude

Thanks to the wonderful influence of my mother, I have grown up as a spiritual person. Not necessarily religious, but very aware of the Universe and all it's wonders. I am humble enough to know that nobody owes me a living and that my journey through life is down to the many choices I make.

I have become aware that the voices inside my head, are a prompting from the Universe as to which direction I need to go. I ignore them at my peril. Countless times, I have been saved from going off on a potentially damaging tangent by cultivating the ability to listen. Gratitude is the language of the universe. It is:

- How we appreciate the Universe and all its wonders
- How we express our appreciation and thanks to others for their acts of love.
- Random acts of kindness we perform to show people that the Universe loves them.
- How we feel about all those who have helped us on our journey
- How we inspire others to be aware of all the gifts they have received
- How we never take anything or anybody for granted
- How we evolve to be in our truth and at peace with ourselves
- Is how we measure our contribution to others
- Gratitude is at the heart of everything we think, say or do. It is not an optional extra.

GRATITUDE LOG

DATE :

- ___
- ___
- ___

DATE :

- ___
- ___
- ___

DATE :

- ___
- ___
- ___

DATE :

- ___
- ___
- ___

DATE :

- ___
- ___
- ___

Most of us gravitate towards selfishly focusing on ourselves. We evaluate people and situations by what they can do for us. On top of that, our ego can make us feel entitled or deserving. When we don't get what we want, we can get angry. All of this can push people away from us and leave us with less, not more.

A true *Attitude of Gratitude*, generates the complete opposite. It is said that 'the only way to get somebody to do anything, is if they **want** to do it' All you need to do is to create the desire.

You can take a horse to water but you cannot make him drink. However, you can put salt in his oats to make him thirsty!

Acts of gratitude are like putting salt in the oats. It makes people thirsty and respond with expressions of gratitude themselves. It then becomes an upward spiral, rather than a decend into the mire of negativity.

Have you noticed how a group of people in a Pub try and outdo themselves by sharing the bad things that have happened to them – the Pity Party!

Developing an *Attitude of Gratitude* doesn't happen overnight. It takes tiny steps repeated day after day for as long as it takes to become a habit. It also takes a heightened state of awareness to understand where to give and where to receive.

Moses Nalocca

MORE Gratitude Less Stress

FUTURE SELF

Describe What The Best Version Of Me Look Like

Things I Have Accomplished That I'm Proud Of

When I Nest Read This, I Hope T Have Travelled To

What Is The Best Part Of My Life

Learned	Enjoy	Grateful

Since you cannot do good to all, you are to pay special attention to those who, by the accidents of time, or place, or circumstances, are brought into closer connection with you.

Saint Augustine

The Danger of Pseudo-Gratitude

Every currency has the potential for being devalued. Language is one of them. There is no point in saying anything unless it is genuine and from the heart. If it is not, whatever you say will do more damage than good. In some parts of the world, you can see two people having a blazing row and then part with the words, "Have a nice day!" It is obviously not meant and has just become a meaningless habit. Speaking without thinking is dangerous. If you are not being genuine with what you say, it is better not to talk. People instinctively know when you mean what you say, and when you don't. Never express gratitude, or indeed say anything, when you don't mean it or if it is just a habit. 'Missing you already?' I dont think so!

Have you noticed the way some companies try to systemise recognition. They have processes for it described in their operations manual. They believe that these will make their staff feel recognised and appreciated. They are wrong. It is false and ineffective.

For example, a business might have a "gratitude wall" with the pictures of their employees, with an award title like "Employee of the Month". Does it mean anything? Is it genuine? Is it motivational or effective? Probably not! It is only there in order to make the customers think that the management actually cares!

If you want to make people feel special, then your recognition to them has to be personal. There is no better way than to face somebody and look them in the eyes and and to say 'thank you' and how much you appreciate them. You don't need any trophies or certificates to do that! You just need to mean it!

There is no such thing as artificial gratitude. Don't settle for anything less than the real thing.

Real gratitude needs to be personal, not given out to a group from the stage. Group recognition becomes so diluted that it vanishes before it gets close to the people it is aimed at.

Gratitude should be a pleasant surprise. If possible, it should also be in-writing so they can share it with their family and friends.

> Start living now.
> Stop saving the good china
> for that special occasion.
> Stop withholding your love
> until that special person materializes.
> Every day you are alive is
> a special occasion.
> Every minute, every breath,
> is a gift from God.
>
> Mary Manin Morrissey

How can you demonstrate your gratitude in a genuine way?

GRATITUDE JOURNAL

DATE _____   S M T W T F S

TODAY I AM GRATEFUL FOR

TODAY'S TOP 3 INTENTIONS

DAILY WATER TRACKER

DAILY FOOD TRACKER

WHAT I AM LEARNING

I LIKE ABOUT MYSELF

NOTES

Seize the Moment!

Life is too short to drink the house-wine, when there are so many glorious vintages to enjoy. There is never going to be enough time to try them all. Live now!

As we go through life, behind us are the quiet clicks of the closing doors we will never open again. Looking back will do us no good. We have to appreciate everyone and everything that is in our lives right now. Be grateful for it. We all experienced Covid, when overnight, all doors closed. Lockdown shut business, it stopped us going out to see family and friends. All our plans, holiday trips and even going into the office, suddenly stopped. Who is to say it could not happen again?

Be grateful for every little thing that happens to you today. Be grateful for every person you meet. Make the most of that moment. Who knows how important that conversation might be. Live in the present. It is a present!

Don't dwell on what went wrong. Instead, focus on what to do next. Spend your energies on moving forward toward finding the answer.

Denis Waitley

What aspect of your life are you most grateful for right now?

Grateful for Fear

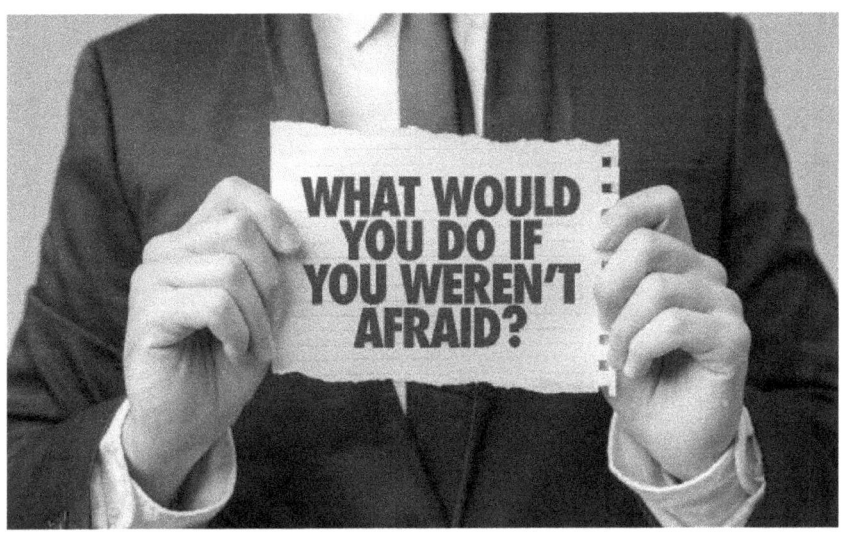

Fear is not a pleasant experience but it is also something to be grateful for. It is a powerful experiece that we can use to lean more about ourselves, and also to become stronger as a result.

What is fear? False Evidence Appearing Real! The truth is that 99% of the things I personally was afraid of at some point, didn't happen. And if you went back in time, I am sure you would come up with the same insight.

Fear is actually a product of your brain which is designed to protect you. Everything that is new, challenging or out of the ordinary frightens you because you don't know how to manage it...yet. When fear comes in, it paralyses you and makes you unable to move forward. But even though it tastes, smells and feels real, it is just an illusion.

So how to deal with it:

- Don't ignore the fear, acknowledge its presence.

- Accept it and allow yourself to work through it.

- Ask your brain: 'Is there a different way I can handle this situation?

Keep in mind that everybody is scared of something and fear is actually not a bad thing. It is a ringing bell which alarms you that there is a decision you have to take, a thing you need to change.

When you go through the 3-step process your brain will align with better solutions and it will provide you new ways to overcome fear. But what happens if you do nothing? Well, fear turns into suffering.

So feel the fear and do it anyway.

Let me know: What are your fears? What is your process of accepting them? What questions do you ask your brain?

Be Grateful for still being in the game!

Yes, life is hard. Being present and doing your duties every single day is hard. And because it's hard, you are in the right place. You need to stay in the game no matter how difficult it gets. That's the key to success.

You are in the queue of life. It's as though that solution, that desire or that dream is not coming true. You wonder why things are not moving, why they aren't changing. Stop asking why. Start asking: Who do I have to become in order to overcome this situation and move forward?

Remember that quitting is not an option. Once you leave the queue, you'll lose the position you reached so far and you'll have to start back again from the beginning. So stay there no matter hard it is. But why should you keep enduring that? Because that's the only way to advance in life.

Do you have a vision that inspires you to stay in the queue? If you have nothing, you'll end up being lazy, being a procrastinator, being a quitter. So find something that makes you wake up with excitement. Make the best out of every day on a regular basis.

Stay in the game not because of what you will get at the end, but because of the person you will become during the process. And yes, this may be common sense but is it common practise? Are you applying it in your life or you think it is just a bunch of beautiful philosophical words? Don't wish things were easier, wish that you were stronger.

Share with me, please: What is the reason you are in the queue? What are you waiting for? Write it down!

Someone's opinion should not become your reality

We are often being taught to pay more attention to our limitations than to our potential. Maybe while you were growing up people were not encouraging you, or not supporting your dreams. Maybe while you were sharing your ideas, people were laughing at you. Maybe they were saying: 'Who do you think you are? What do you think is so special about you?'

Well, let me tell you something. You are special for sure. And not because I compare you to another person, but because of the fact that every human is unique and has greatness. It's time for you to see yourself as a truly amazing being, to rise above your limitations. You need to explore your potential. Keep in mind that whenever someone points your limitations out, it's not because you can't do something, but because they see their own limitations and want to reflect them on you. Don't blame them, forgive them. Just set yourself apart from people who bring you down and decide who you prefer to be around.

Someone's opinion should never become your reality.
Stop playing small and trying to please people. Start thinking about what you can learn, what you can contribute, what you need to change in order to live up to your true potential. Other people's opinions don't matter. Only your own does. Be grateful for that!

An attitude of gratitude builds your confidence

The one common word that is crucial to both confidence and performance is certainty. If you break down the word confidence in Latin, it is "con fiducia", which means 'with trust.' You need to have absolute trust in yourself and absolute trust in something, which could be your business, project or venture. Certainty, absolute trust and absolute belief will help you develop your skills in confidence and performance.

One way you can build your confidence is by always keeping your word, not only to other people but to yourself as well. So, when you say you are going to do something, or you are going to work on something, keep your word and follow through with it. If you say to yourself, "Tomorrow I am going to the gym," then you must do it. The consequence of not going to the gym is much more serious than simply a missed workout. The real consequence is self-doubt, as even your own brain doesn't trust you anymore because you didn't keep your word

Obviously, this will have an immense effect on the way you perform. Whenever you have to take a big step or a big action, your brain will tell you, "Hey, you didn't even keep your word when you said you were going to the gym.

How can I now support you in this harder and more complex task?"

Another way of building confidence is to work and grow your mindset. Invest more time working on yourself, your projects, and your business, as this will build muscle confidence. The more you choose to believe in yourself and spend time on yourself, the easier it will become and the more confident you will feel. It is like going to the gym; you can't build your biceps without lifting weights repeatedly

One thing which is essential to remember is that there will bemoments when your confidence and performance are affected and when you listen to the naysayers. Ignore those who doubt you because they will always have something to say about you.

Make sure you look at what you have already achieved; this will always motivate you and push you to perform in a better way. Focusing on past achievements is extremely effective because you have done it already, so your brain has references for what has been done and what you have experienced. Take some time to practice gratitude.

Be grateful for what you have, what you have achieved and what is coming ahead.

Moses Nalocca

Gratitude first and last

When I started working on this book on Gratitude I realised how important appreciation has been in my life. So many of the things, people and opportunities that have come my way would have steered well clear of me without it.

When I look round at everything I have, I cannot fail to be hugely grateful.

Gratitude is the highest form of consciousness. Through gratitude, we get access to our Creator and the Universe, whatever that means to you. This is not about religion, it is about the simple acknowledgement that there is something bigger out there than ourselves. Recognising the spiritual aspect to our lives adds a new and exciting dimension to everything.

> *No one who achieves success does so without acknowledging the help of others. The wise and confident acknowledge this help with gratitude.*
>
> *Alfred North Whitehead*

Gratitude is the key to how you remove any type of selfishness. It is no longer just about you. It allows you to become a co-creator of circumstances along with your Creator. One of the first things for you to be able attract more in your life is to develop an attitude, where being grateful is a fundamental part of your life. Because you get in life, not what you want, but what you are. The more you're grateful, the more the universe will want to create more with you. You become part of the co-creation.

When I am working with my athletes, and clients, I task them every day with focussing on three things they are deeply grateful for. This is a great habit to get in to! The moment you focus on those three things that you are grateful for, you expand, and you get into a new dimension.

When I do this myself, I realise that I am rich in so many ways. Being rich is nothing to do with money. I am abundant. I feel healthy. The more you are aware of that, the more you vibrate in those frequencies, the more you attract into your world.

As with every aspect of improving ourselves, developing this attitude is something you need to work on every day. This is what I call conditioning. You need to condition yourself. It's not about reading one book and believing that you have you have learned that lesson for life. Anything worthwhile needs to be worked on everyday.

The trouble with things that are easy to do, is that they are also easy NOT to do. Unless we consciously turn things into a habit, other things will get in the way. Distractions are everywhere!

When I am coaching professional athletes, they are training every single day. No matter how long they have been in their particular sport, I insist that they practice the basics every single day. The amateur practices till they get it right. The professional practices till thay cannot get it wrong! Practicing your attitude of gratitude is one of those fundamentals.

Some people say to me that they don't have anything to be grateful for. That would be so sad if it were true. But it is not. They are simply allowing the negative things in their life to eclipse all of the many positives things that might be hidden from them at that moment.

At the very least, all of us can be grateful for our parents, or whoever raised us, and gave us the education that enabled us to read. This gave us the ability to learn and grow.

Be thankful that you live in a free country and have the ability to make choices for your future.

Take nothing for granted! Everything is a gift.

Gratitude can transform
common days into thanksgivings,
turn routine jobs into joy,
and change ordinary opportunities
into blessings.

William Arthur Ward

Gratitude is the magnet that will attract more to you every day.

Take a moment to look around you in your circle of family and friends. I am sure you will not have to look far to find someone who is miserable and complaining. They don't smile. They don't laugh, they are stuck in a bubble of gloom of their own making. Their focus is on materialistic things, mainly those they don't have. Their only interest is in themselves and dragging those around them down to their level.

Compare those to who you like to be around. The people who smile when they see you. Those who are genuinely interested in you and what is happening in your life. They are easy to talk to. They laugh often and are always appreciative, and supportive. They don't complain or criticise and always put others needs before their own. Which would you like to spend more time with?

Your attitude and the way you think, is expressed by the words you use when talking to the people around you. Your ready smile, your willingness to listen and to look for ways of helping. The spark inside you can light up a room or a country. It is how you choose to use it.

Tony Buzan, the inventor of Mind Mapping, was known for reacting to challenging events by saying "How fascinating!" He would never react with a negative word. It is your fundamental attitude to every situation that you will be known for. And everything is connected!

Give yourself a gift of
five minutes of contemplation
in awe of everything
you see around you.
Go outside and turn your
attention to the many
miracles
around you.
This five-minute-a-day
regimen of appreciation
and gratitude will help
you to focus your life in awe.

Wayne Dyer

Developing your attitude is just like developing a muscle, you have to work on it every day.

In every situation, before reacting to it, there is a millisecond of decision making time in which you can choose how you are going to react. When I discovered this it changed my life. Like it or not, we are all pre-programmed on how to react in any given situation.

When something goes wrong we get annoyed. It is natural. However, it is our choice of how we express that negative emotion. We can react or we can choose not to react. Whichever we choose will have a consequence. It will influence those around us one way or another.

In London's West End there are plays and musicals taking place every night. No matter which day you go to see a show, you know you can rely on a perfect performance from each of the cast members. They will be energetic, funny, positive and totally professional at every performance.

Does that mean for the rest of the day, they exhibit those same qualities? Certainly not! They are human beings, not robots! However, a skill that they have developed is the art of total focus and living in the moment. It is called "Theatrical Flair. It is the ability to assume a role for a particular purpose. It is a choice and a valuable skill whether you are on stage as a performer, or assuming the role of a manager in front of your employees.

I believe our greatest source of inspiration is to observe the actions and the words of others.

Gratitude is one of the strongest
and most transformative
states of being.
It shifts your perspective
from lack to abundance
and allows you to focus on
the good in your life,
which in turn pulls more
goodness into your reality.

Jen Sincero

Radiating Gratitude

During this book, I have described the different ways that Gratitude has impacted on my life and changed my outlook. Of course, this is an internal state. When you discover how to radiate Gratitude, is when you massively increase the impace you have on others.

It is the difference between receiving and giving. Create a new habit of reviewing each day and indentifying those people who impacted you in a special way. Now, share with them the gratitude you feel for them in a tangible way. I am not saying you should send them flowers, as this may not be appropriate. What you can do is to send them a short text, email, voice message or post, to say thank you. It really has an impact.

The other powerful thing is when you share gratiude about somebody in a public forum, such as social media. For them to see you congratulating them in public is the ultimate recognition.

The universe has a wonderful way of bringing people into our lives to help teach us life's great lessons. One thing is for certain, there is no such thing as coincidence. We are all exactly where we are meant to be at every moment and are all a part of a great divine plan.

No one who achieves
success does so without
acknowledging
the help of others.
The wise and confident
acknowledge this help
with gratitude.

Alfred North Whitehead

For this Gratitude Journal to have any value to you, I suggest making an entry in it everyday. Write down the achievements you are proud of, the good things that happened and the people who made your day special. Make adding these to your journal, a habit! On those days when you are challenged or when something negative happens, it can be very encouraging to be able to refer back to those good memories in order to get a positive boost.

This book is where you should look to find them. If you use it well, it will become a permenant source of positive inspiration.

Thanks for reading!

Thankfulness is the beginning of gratitude. Gratitude is the completion of thankfulness. Thankfulness may consist merely of words. Gratitude is shown in acts.

Henri Frederic Amiel

Resources

Let me invite you to join the,

MORE:
Official Moses Nalocca Community

https://www.facebook.com/mosesnalocca

https://www.instagram.com/mosesnalocca/

https://twitter.com/mjnalocca?lang=en

https://www.linkedin.com/in/mosesjnalocca/

https://www.youtube.com/channel/UC8uomzdjPu2Bai_e4M0kMfw

www.ingramcontent.com/pod-product-compliance
Lightning Source LLC
Chambersburg PA
CBHW041143110526
44590CB00027B/4108